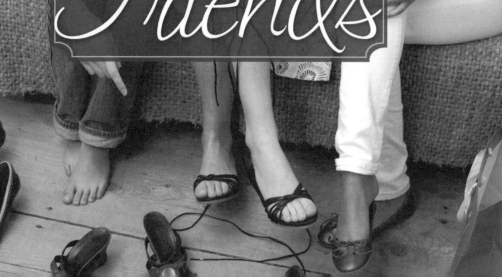

INSPIRAT

Friends

Compiled by Rebecca Germany.

ISBN 978-1-60260-199-4

Some material previously published in *365 Favorite Quotes for Friends*, *365 Treasured Moments for Sisters*, *A Heartfelt Thanks*, and *Wishing You Happy Birthday*. All published by Barbour Publishing, Inc.

Quotations without credit are by Rebecca Germany.

Scripture quotations marked KJV are taken from the King James Version of the Bible.

Scripture quotations marked NIV are taken from the HOLY BIBLE, NEW INTERNATIONAL VERSION®. NIV®. Copyright © 1973, 1978, 1984 by International Bible Society. Used by permission of Zondervan. All rights reserved.

Scripture quotations marked NRSV are taken from the New Revised Standard Version Bible, copyright 1989, Division of Christian Education the National Council of the Churches of Christ in the United States of America. Used by permission. All rights reserved.

Scripture quotations marked NLT are taken from the *Holy Bible,* New Living Translation, copyright © 1996. Used by permission of Tyndale House Publishers, Inc. Wheaton, Illinois 60189, U.S.A. All rights reserved.

Scripture quotations marked MSG are from ***THE MESSAGE.*** Copyright © by Eugene H. Peterson 1993, 1994, 1995, 1996, 2000, 2001, 200 Used by permission of NavPress Publishing Group.

Cover Photograph: Kay Blaschke/Stock 4B/Getty Images

Published by Barbour Publishing, Inc., P.O. Box 719, Uhrichsville, Ohio 44683, www.barbourbooks.com

Our mission is to publish and distribute inspirational products offering exceptional value and biblical encouragement to the masses.

INSPIRATION FOR

Friends

BARBOUR

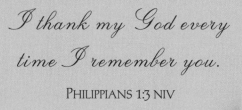

I thank my God every time I remember you.

PHILIPPIANS 1:3 NIV

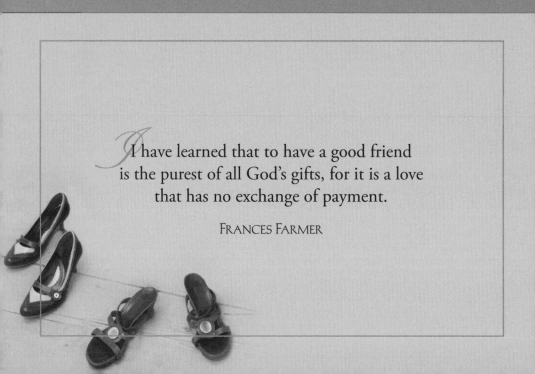

I have learned that to have a good friend
is the purest of all God's gifts, for it is a love
that has no exchange of payment.

FRANCES FARMER

The best mirror is an old friend.

GEORGE HERBERT

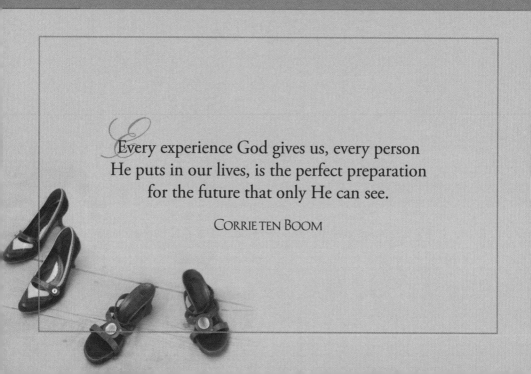

Every experience God gives us, every person
He puts in our lives, is the perfect preparation
for the future that only He can see.

CORRIE TEN BOOM

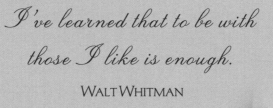

I've learned that to be with those I like is enough.

WALT WHITMAN

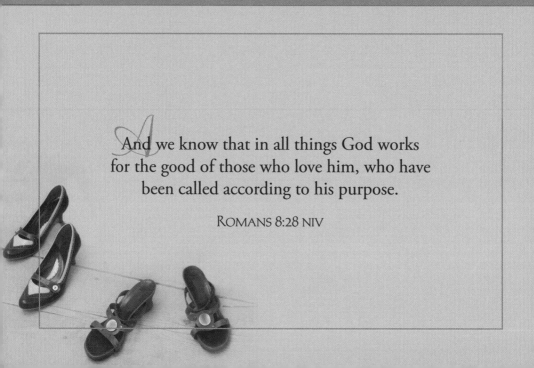

And we know that in all things God works
for the good of those who love him, who have
been called according to his purpose.

ROMANS 8:28 NIV

The language of friendship is not words, but meanings. It is an intelligence above language.

HENRY DAVID THOREAU

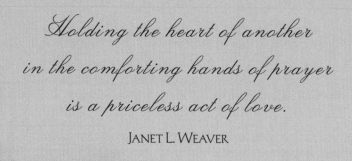

Holding the heart of another
in the comforting hands of prayer
is a priceless act of love.

JANET L. WEAVER

Every man should have a fair-sized cemetery
in which to bury the faults of his friends.

HENRY WARD BEECHER

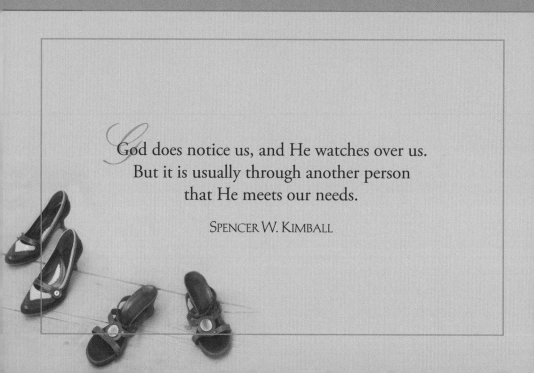

God does notice us, and He watches over us.
But it is usually through another person
that He meets our needs.

SPENCER W. KIMBALL

Friendship is the inexpressible comfort of feeling safe with a person, having neither to weigh thoughts nor measure words.

George Eliot

The best things in life are never rationed.
Friendship, loyalty, love do not require coupons.

GEORGE T. HEWITT

Friendship is the breathing rose

with sweets in every fold.

OLIVER WENDELL HOLMES

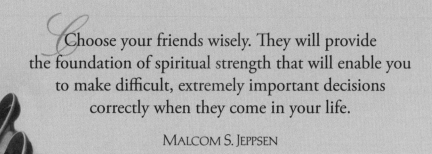

Choose your friends wisely. They will provide
the foundation of spiritual strength that will enable you
to make difficult, extremely important decisions
correctly when they come in your life.

MALCOM S. JEPPSEN

No friendship can cross the path of our destiny without leaving some mark on it forever.

François Mauriac

A friend loveth at all times.

PROVERBS 17:17 KJV

There are kind hearts still for friends to fill.

ROBERT LOUIS STEVENSON

The finger of God touches your life
when you make a friend.

MARY DAWSON HUGHES

*Verily, great grace may go with a little gift;
and precious are all things that come from friends.*

THEOCRITUS

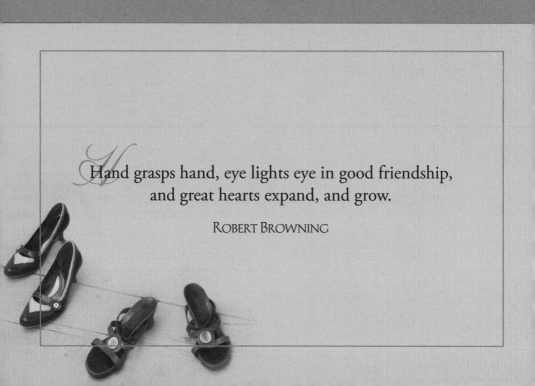

Hand grasps hand, eye lights eye in good friendship,
and great hearts expand, and grow.

ROBERT BROWNING

The road to a friend's house is never long.

DANISH PROVERB

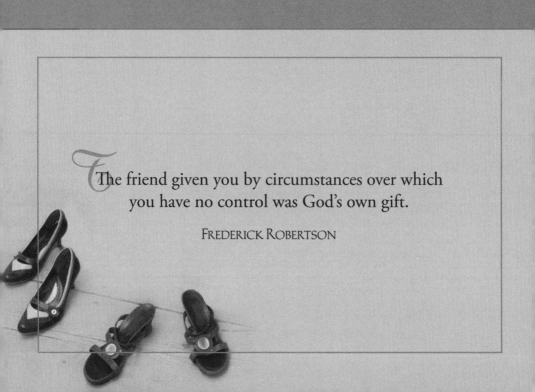

The friend given you by circumstances over which
you have no control was God's own gift.

FREDERICK ROBERTSON

Friendship without self-interest is one of the rare and beautiful things in life.

<small>JAMES FRANCIS BYRNES</small>

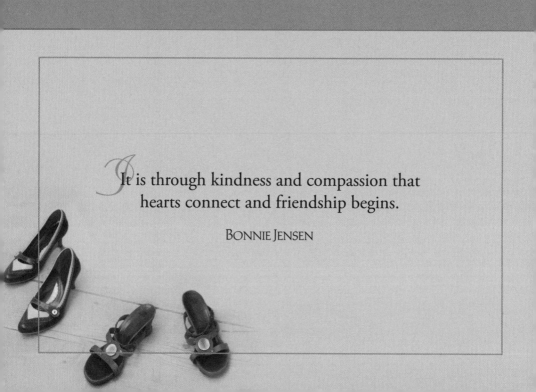

It is through kindness and compassion that
hearts connect and friendship begins.

BONNIE JENSEN

The greatest sweetener of human life is friendship.

JOSEPH ADDISON

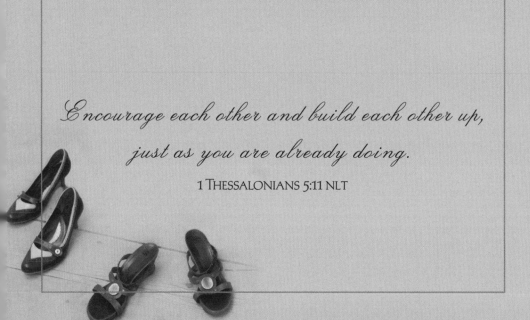

Encourage each other and build each other up,
just as you are already doing.

1 Thessalonians 5:11 NLT

A real friend warms you by his presence, trusts you with his secrets, and remembers you in his prayers.

UNKNOWN

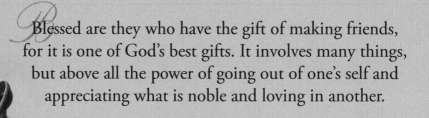

Blessed are they who have the gift of making friends,
for it is one of God's best gifts. It involves many things,
but above all the power of going out of one's self and
appreciating what is noble and loving in another.

THOMAS HUGHES

Loyalty is what we seek in friendship.

CICERO

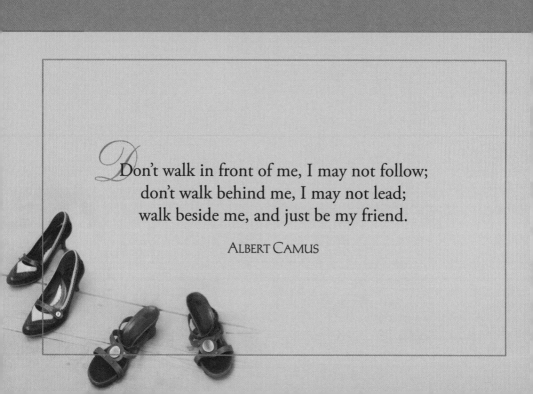

Don't walk in front of me, I may not follow;
don't walk behind me, I may not lead;
walk beside me, and just be my friend.

ALBERT CAMUS

Friendship. . .a union of spirits,

a marriage of hearts.

WILLIAM PENN

Be devoted to one another in brotherly love.

Honor one another above yourselves.

ROMANS 12:10 NIV

*I*ndeed, we do not really live unless
we have friends surrounding us like a firm
wall against the winds of the world.

CHARLES HANSON TOWNE

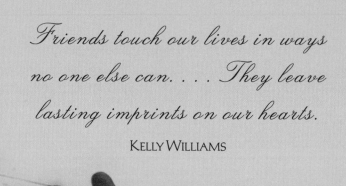

Friends touch our lives in ways no one else can. . . . They leave lasting imprints on our hearts.

KELLY WILLIAMS

To know someone here or there with whom
you can feel there is understanding in spite of
differences or thoughts expressed. . .
that can make life a garden.

JOHANN WOLFGANG VON GOETHE

*Never shall I forget the days
which I spent with you.*

LUDWIG VAN BEETHOVEN

No one has ever seen God; but if we love one another,
God lives in us and his love is made complete in us.

1 JOHN 4:12 NIV

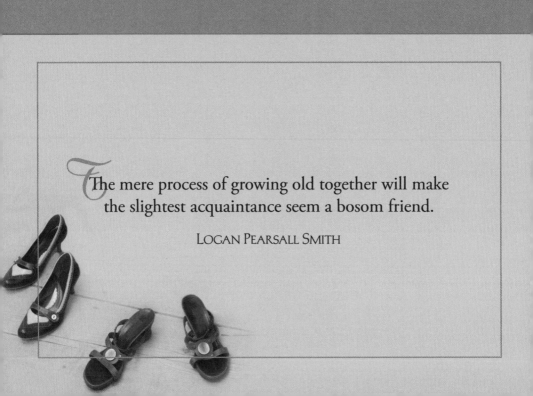

The mere process of growing old together will make
the slightest acquaintance seem a bosom friend.

LOGAN PEARSALL SMITH

The joy that you give to others
is the joy that comes back to you.

JOHN GREENLEAF WHITTIER

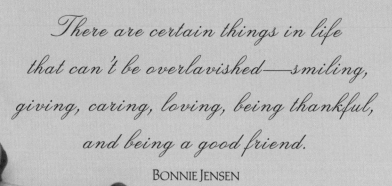

*There are certain things in life
that can't be overlavished—smiling,
giving, caring, loving, being thankful,
and being a good friend.*

BONNIE JENSEN

Knowing you has added another square
to the quilt of my life. The fabric is stamped with
your unique touch. The pieces are woven with the
memories of our time together. The stitching is firm,
binding our friendship for eternity.

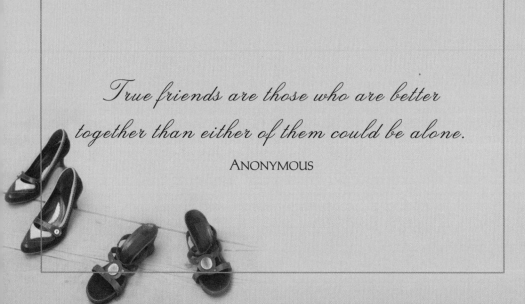

True friends are those who are better together than either of them could be alone.

ANONYMOUS

What a great blessing is a friend with a heart so trusty you may safely bury all your secrets in it.

SENECA

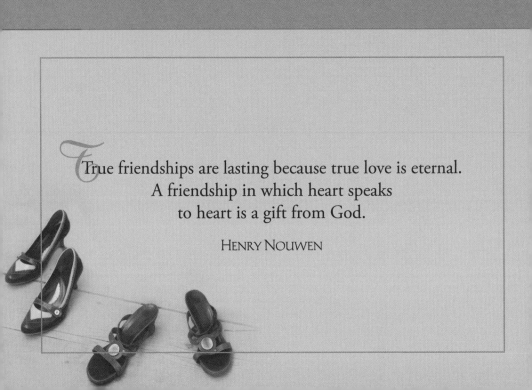

True friendships are lasting because true love is eternal.
A friendship in which heart speaks
to heart is a gift from God.

HENRY NOUWEN

One enemy is too many;
a hundred friends too few.

ANONYMOUS

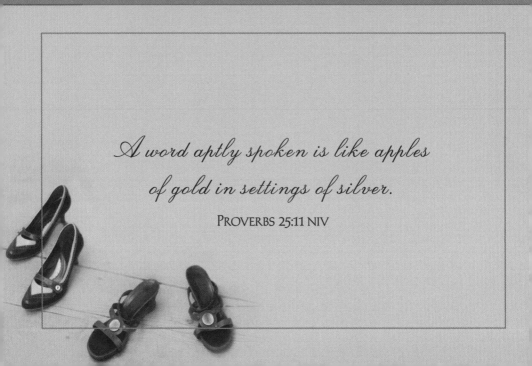

A word aptly spoken is like apples of gold in settings of silver.

PROVERBS 25:11 NIV

I no doubt deserved my enemies,
but I don't believe I deserved my friends.

WALT WHITMAN

Only the virtuous have friends.

VOLTAIRE

$\mathcal{A}$ friend is a person with whom I may be sincere.
Before him I may think aloud.

RALPH WALDO EMERSON

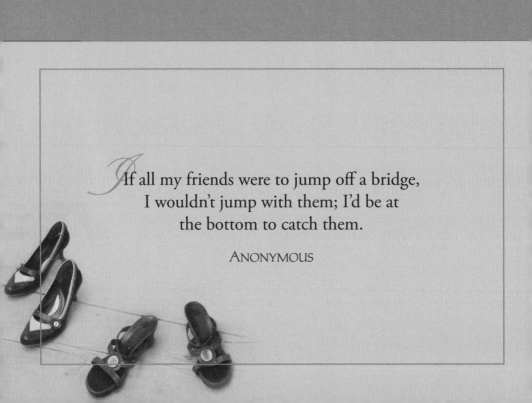

If all my friends were to jump off a bridge,
I wouldn't jump with them; I'd be at
the bottom to catch them.

ANONYMOUS

Friends have all things in common.

GREEK PROVERB

Be encouraged and knit together
by strong ties of love.

COLOSSIANS 2:2 NLT

One good friend is not to be weighed
against all the jewels of the earth.

WILL CARLETON

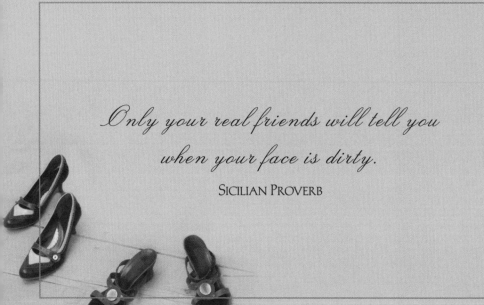

Only your real friends will tell you when your face is dirty.

SICILIAN PROVERB

Trouble is the sieve through which
we sift our acquaintances. Those too big to pass
through are our friends.

ARLENE FRANCIS

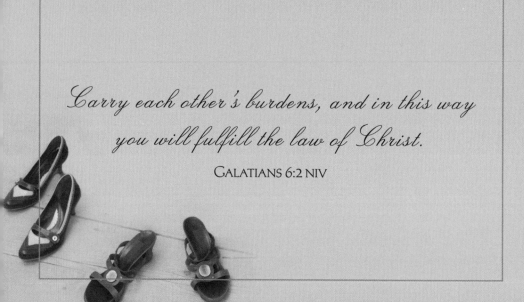

Carry each other's burdens, and in this way you will fulfill the law of Christ.

GALATIANS 6:2 NIV

The best that we find in our travels is an honest friend.
He is a fortunate voyager who finds many.

ROBERT LOUIS STEVENSON

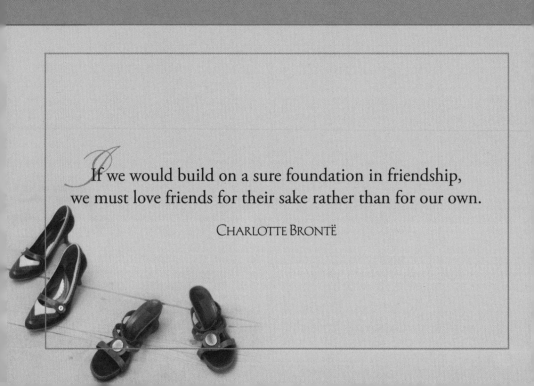

*If we would build on a sure foundation in friendship,
we must love friends for their sake rather than for our own.*

CHARLOTTE BRONTË

Insomuch as any one pushes you nearer to God, he or she is your friend.

FRENCH PROVERB

Some people come into our lives,

leave footprints on our hearts,

and we are never the same.

UNKNOWN

When I have opened my heart to a friend,
I am more myself than ever.

THOMAS MOORE

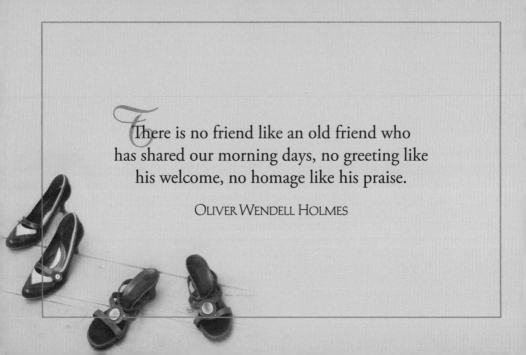

There is no friend like an old friend who has shared our morning days, no greeting like his welcome, no homage like his praise.

OLIVER WENDELL HOLMES

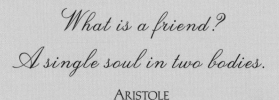

What is a friend?
A single soul in two bodies.

ARISTOLE

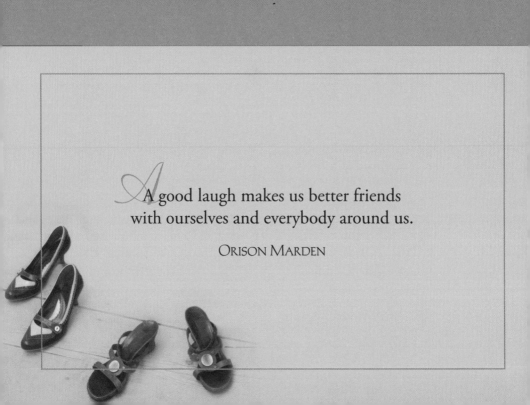

A good laugh makes us better friends
with ourselves and everybody around us.

ORISON MARDEN

Do not protect yourself by a fence,

but rather by your friends.

CZECH PROVERB

Trust should be in God, who richly gives us all we need for our enjoyment.

1 TIMOTHY 6:17 NLT

A true friend is someone who is there for you
when he'd rather be anywhere else.

LEN WEIN

I thank You,
God in heaven, for friends.

MARGARET SANGSTER

'Tis the privilege of friendship to talk nonsense, and have her nonsense respected.

CHARLES LAMB

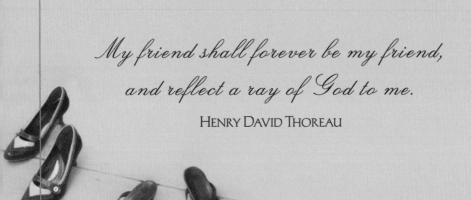

My friend shall forever be my friend,

and reflect a ray of God to me.

HENRY DAVID THOREAU

There was a definite process by which one made people into friends, and it involved talking to them and listening to them for hours at a time.

REBECCA WEST

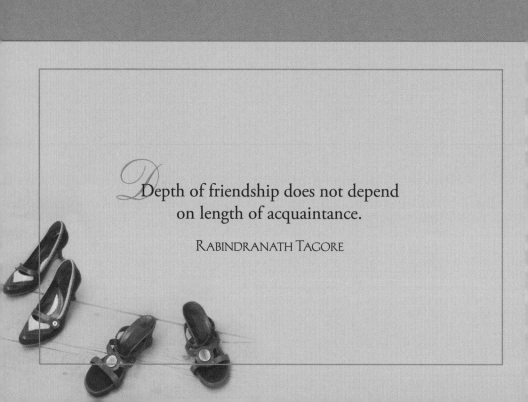

Depth of friendship does not depend
on length of acquaintance.

RABINDRANATH TAGORE

When you're with a friend,
your heart has come home.

EMILY FARBER

The greatest healing therapy

is friendship and love.

HUBERT HUMPHREY

A friend is someone who knows the song
in your heart and can sing it back to you
when you have forgotten the words.

UNKNOWN

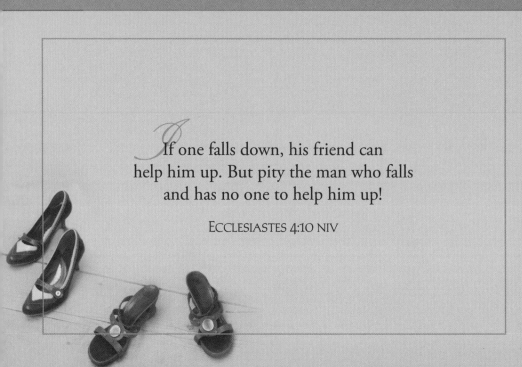

If one falls down, his friend can
help him up. But pity the man who falls
and has no one to help him up!

ECCLESIASTES 4:10 NIV

A true friend is the gift of God and. . .
He only who made hearts can unite them.

ROBERT SOUTH

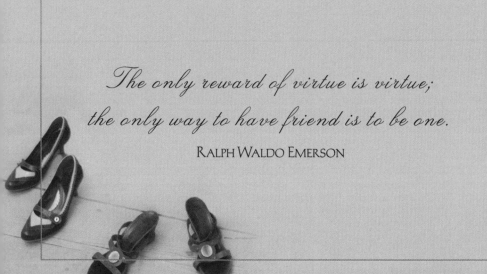

*The only reward of virtue is virtue;
the only way to have friend is to be one.*

RALPH WALDO EMERSON

$\mathscr{C}$ultivate solitude and quiet and a few
sincere friends, rather than mob merriment, noise,
and thousands of nodding acquaintances.

WILLIAM POWELL

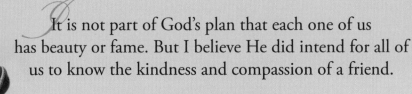

It is not part of God's plan that each one of us
has beauty or fame. But I believe He did intend for all of
us to know the kindness and compassion of a friend.

ANITA WIEGAND

I had three chairs in my house:
one for solitude, two for friendship.

HENRY DAVID THOREAU

Only friends will tell you the truths you need to hear to make the last part of your life bearable.

FRANCINE DU PLESSIX GRAY

My friend is not perfect—nor am I—
and so we suit each other admirably.

ALEXANDER POPE

A real friend helps us think our best thoughts,
do our noblest deeds, be our finest selves.

UNKNOWN

My friends are my estate.

EMILY DICKINSON

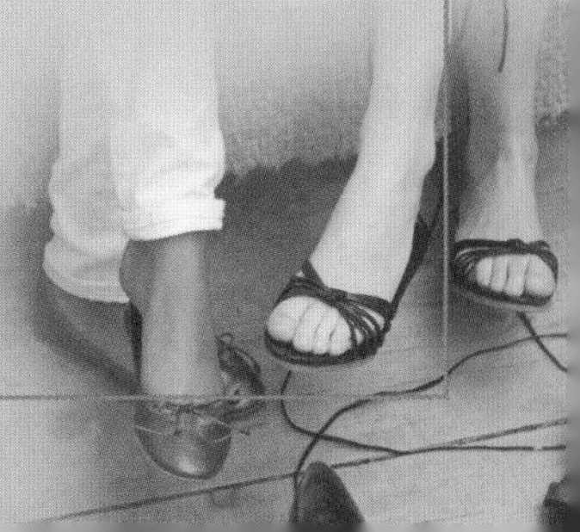

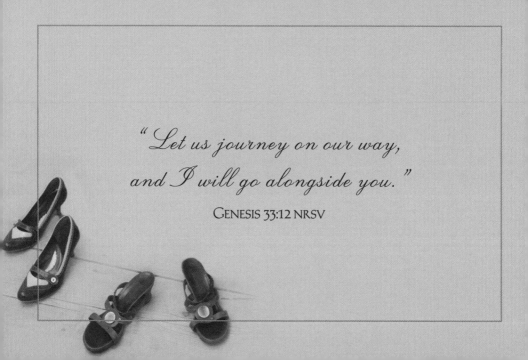

" *Let us journey on our way,
and I will go alongside you.* "

GENESIS 33:12 NRSV

*I*n prosperity our friends know us;
in adversity we know our friends.

CHURTON COLLINS

*I*t's easier to believe in yourself when you have a friend beside you saying, "I believe in you, too."

BONNIE JENSEN

Good company upon the road is the shortest cut.

ANONYMOUS

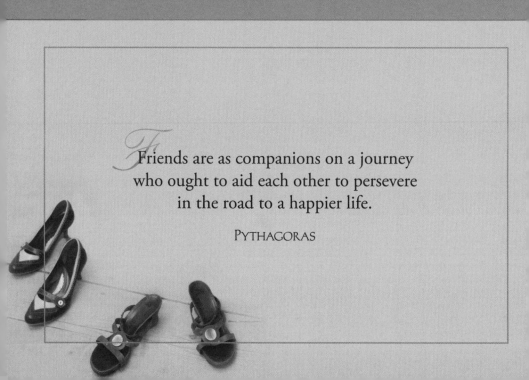

Friends are as companions on a journey
who ought to aid each other to persevere
in the road to a happier life.

PYTHAGORAS

I count myself in nothing else so happy
as in a soul remembering my good friends.

WILLIAM SHAKESPEARE

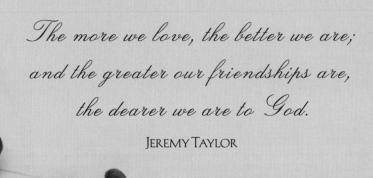

The more we love, the better we are;
and the greater our friendships are,
the dearer we are to God.

JEREMY TAYLOR

As gold more splendid from the fire appears,
thus friendship brightens by the length of years.

THOMAS CARLYLE

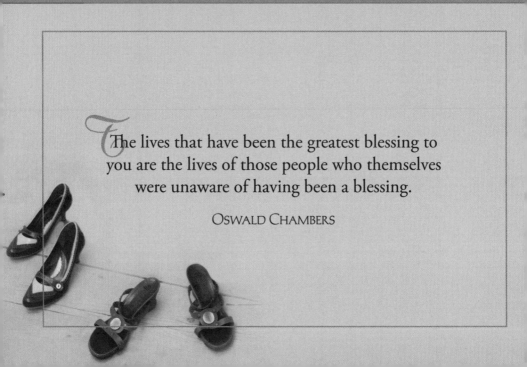

The lives that have been the greatest blessing to you are the lives of those people who themselves were unaware of having been a blessing.

Oswald Chambers

Hold a true friend with both your hands.

NIGERIAN PROVERB

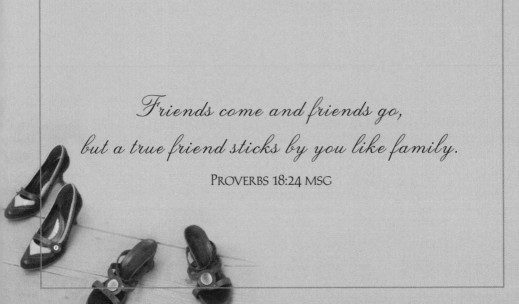

Friends come and friends go,
but a true friend sticks by you like family.

PROVERBS 18:24 MSG

I may have chosen my friends,
but the strength of the bond between us
was beyond my control.

ANITA WIEGAND

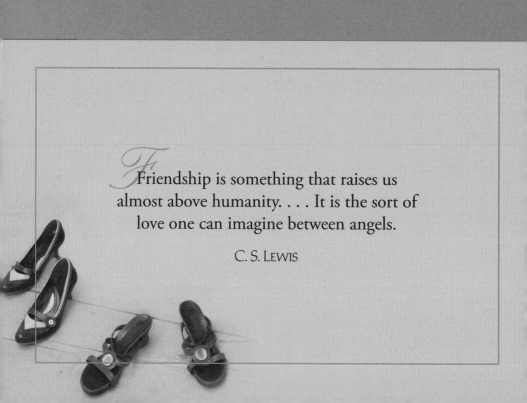

Friendship is something that raises us almost above humanity. . . . It is the sort of love one can imagine between angels.

C. S. LEWIS

A man's growth is seen in the successive choirs of his friends.

RALPH WALDO EMERSON

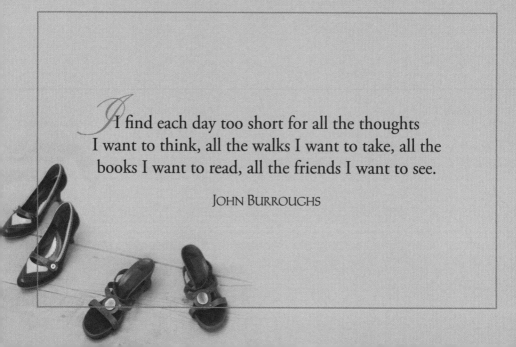

I find each day too short for all the thoughts
I want to think, all the walks I want to take, all the
books I want to read, all the friends I want to see.

JOHN BURROUGHS

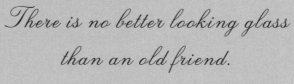

There is no better looking glass

than an old friend.

THOMAS FULLER

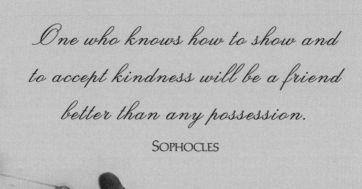

One who knows how to show and to accept kindness will be a friend better than any possession.

SOPHOCLES

Yes, we must ever be friends; and of all who offer you friendship let me be ever the first, the truest, the nearest, and dearest!

HENRY WADSWORTH LONGFELLOW

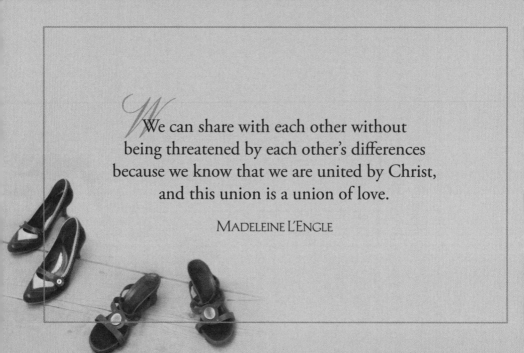

We can share with each other without
being threatened by each other's differences
because we know that we are united by Christ,
and this union is a union of love.

MADELEINE L'ENGLE

Wisdom is enshrined in

an understanding heart.

PROVERBS 14:33 NLT

I don't meddle with what my friends believe or
reject, any more than I ask whether they
are rich or poor; I love them.

JAMES RUSSELL LOWELL

Joy is the net of love by which you can catch souls.

MOTHER TERESA

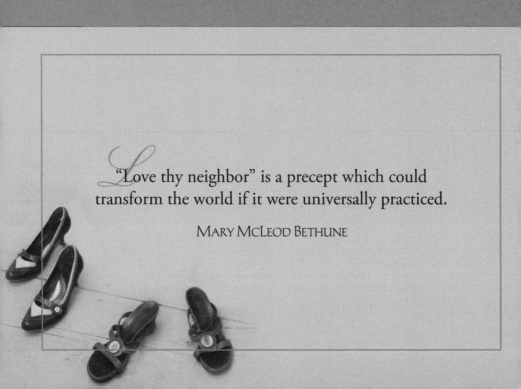

"Love thy neighbor" is a precept which could transform the world if it were universally practiced.

MARY MCLEOD BETHUNE

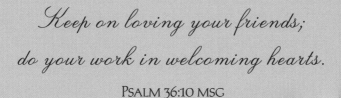

*Keep on loving your friends;
do your work in welcoming hearts.*

PSALM 36:10 MSG

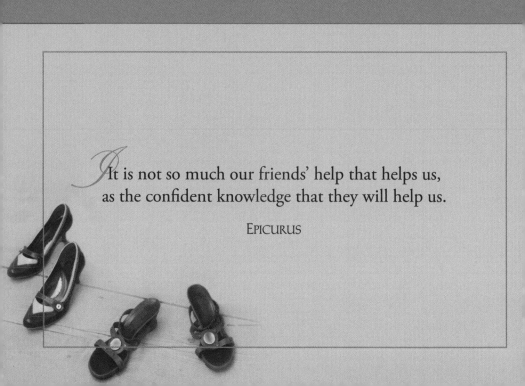

It is not so much our friends' help that helps us,
as the confident knowledge that they will help us.

EPICURUS

Familiar acts are beautiful through love.

PERCY BYSSHE SHELLEY

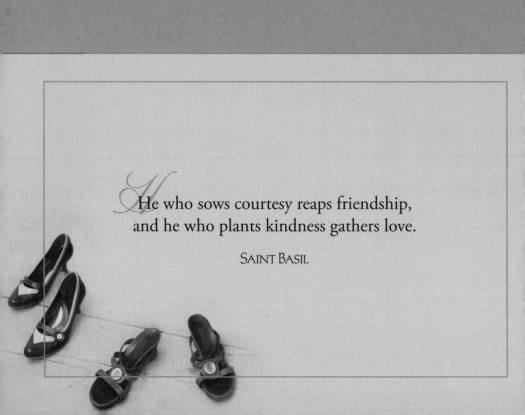

He who sows courtesy reaps friendship,
and he who plants kindness gathers love.

SAINT BASIL

One does not make friends.

One recognizes them.

IRENE DUNN

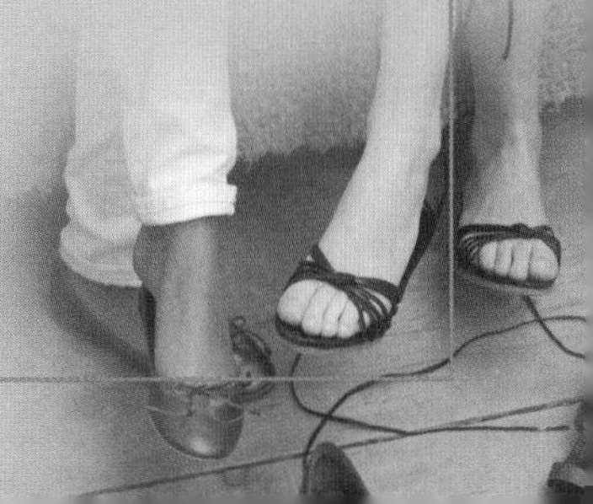

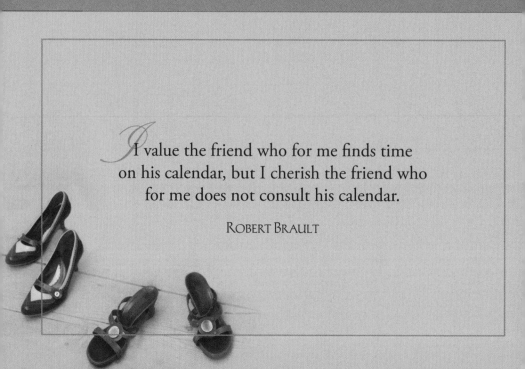

I value the friend who for me finds time on his calendar, but I cherish the friend who for me does not consult his calendar.

ROBERT BRAULT

Life is fortified by many friendships.

SYDNEY SMITH

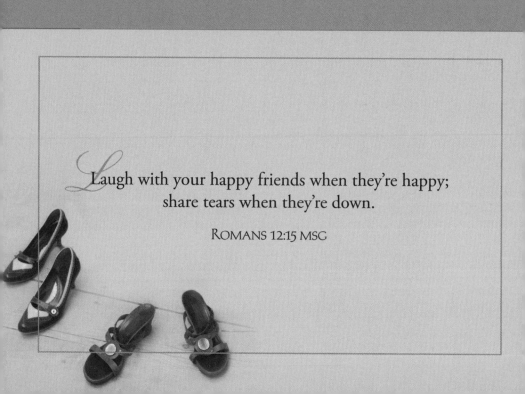

Laugh with your happy friends when they're happy;
share tears when they're down.

ROMANS 12:15 MSG

A friend may well be reckoned

a masterpiece of nature.

RALPH WALDO EMERSON

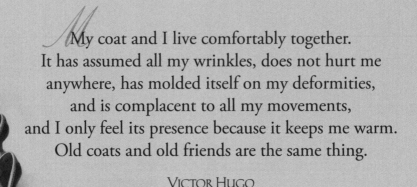

My coat and I live comfortably together.
It has assumed all my wrinkles, does not hurt me
anywhere, has molded itself on my deformities,
and is complacent to all my movements,
and I only feel its presence because it keeps me warm.
Old coats and old friends are the same thing.

VICTOR HUGO

Dear friends, no matter how we find them, are as essential to our lives as breathing in and breathing out.

LOIS WYSE

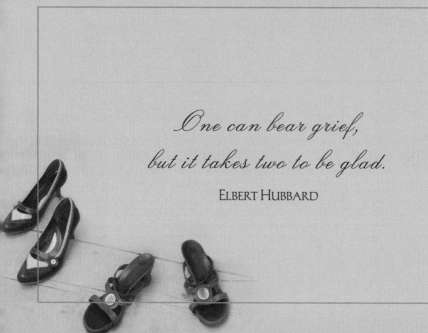

One can bear grief,
but it takes two to be glad.

ELBERT HUBBARD

*B*ut friendship is precious, not only in the shade,
but in the sunshine of life; and thanks to a benevolent
arrangement of things, the greater part of life is sunshine.

THOMAS JEFFERSON

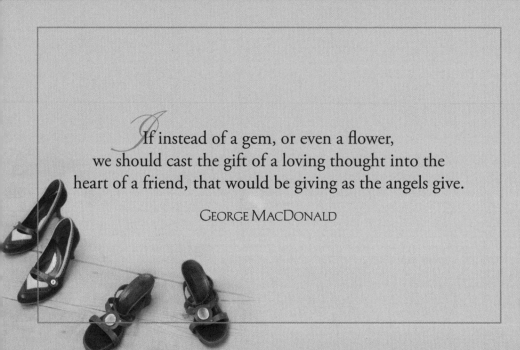

If instead of a gem, or even a flower,
we should cast the gift of a loving thought into the
heart of a friend, that would be giving as the angels give.

GEORGE MACDONALD

*J*ust thinking about a friend makes you want to do a happy dance, because a friend is someone who loves you in spite of your faults.

CHARLES SCHULZ

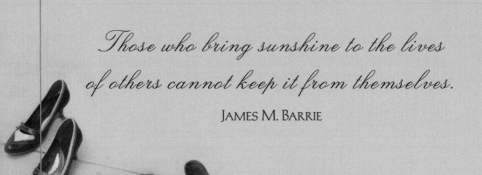

Those who bring sunshine to the lives of others cannot keep it from themselves.

JAMES M. BARRIE

What greater thing is there for human souls
than to feel that they are joined for life—
to be with each other in silent unspeakable memories.

GEORGE ELIOT

*K*eep on loving each other. . . .
Do not forget to entertain strangers, for by so doing
some people have entertained angels without knowing it.

HEBREWS 13:1-2 NIV

*What joy is better than
the news of friends?*

ROBERT BROWNING

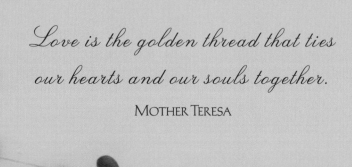

*Love is the golden thread that ties
our hearts and our souls together.*

MOTHER TERESA

$\mathcal{L}$ife is a chronicle of friendship. Friends create the world anew each day. Without their loving care, courage would not suffice to keep hearts strong for life.

HELEN KELLER

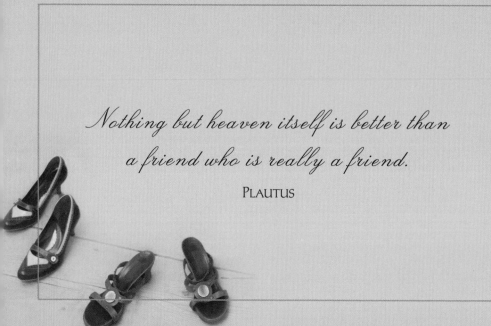

Nothing but heaven itself is better than a friend who is really a friend.

PLAUTUS

*I*t is one of the most beautiful compensations of life, that no man can sincerely try to help another without helping himself.

RALPH WALDO EMERSON

*A*cross the years, we've met in dreams and shared each other's hopes and schemes. We've known a friendship rich and rare and beautiful beyond compare.

*It is in the shelter of
each other that people live.*

IRISH PROVERB

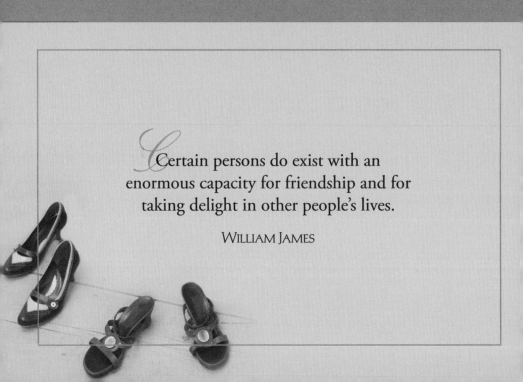

Certain persons do exist with an
enormous capacity for friendship and for
taking delight in other people's lives.

WILLIAM JAMES

Every soul that touches yours—be it the slightest contact—gets there from some good.

GEORGE ELIOT

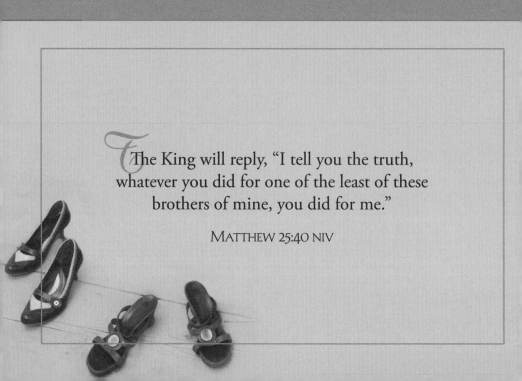

The King will reply, "I tell you the truth, whatever you did for one of the least of these brothers of mine, you did for me."

MATTHEW 25:40 NIV

Let us be grateful to people who make us happy; they are the charming gardeners who make our souls blossom.

MARCEL PROUST

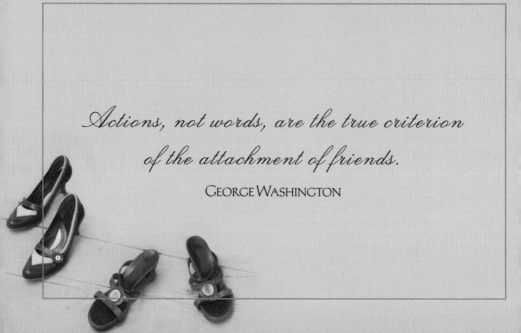

Actions, not words, are the true criterion of the attachment of friends.

GEORGE WASHINGTON

A friend is one to whom one may pour out
all the contents of one's heart, chaff and grain together,
knowing that the gentlest of hands will take and sift it,
keep what is worth keeping and with a breath
of kindness blow the rest away.

ARABIAN PROVERB

*Love is all we have, the only way
that each can help the other.*

EURIPIDES

When we do the best that we can,
we never know what miracle is wrought in our life,
or in the life of another.

HELEN KELLER

Those who bring sunshine to the lives of others cannot keep it from themselves.

JAMES BARRIE

*Laughter is not at all a bad beginning for a friendship,
and it is far the best ending for one.*

Oscar Wilde

Human love and the delights of friendship,
out of which are built the memories that endure, are also
to be treasured up as hints of what shall be hereafter.

BEDE JARRETT

*To love is to place our happiness
in the happiness of another.*

GOTTFRIED WILHELM VON LEIBNIZ

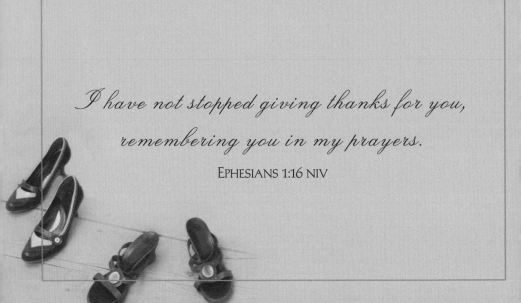

I have not stopped giving thanks for you, remembering you in my prayers.

EPHESIANS 1:16 NIV

Some people weave burlap into the fabric of our lives, and some weave gold thread. Both contribute to make the whole picture beautiful and unique.

UNKNOWN

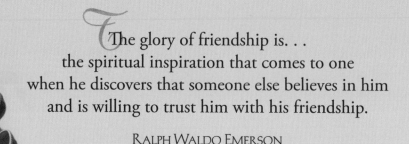

The glory of friendship is. . .
the spiritual inspiration that comes to one
when he discovers that someone else believes in him
and is willing to trust him with his friendship.

RALPH WALDO EMERSON

Over cups of tea, I listened to my friend,
and my friend heard me. My joy was hers and hers was mine,
as we shared our hearts line by line.

ANONYMOUS

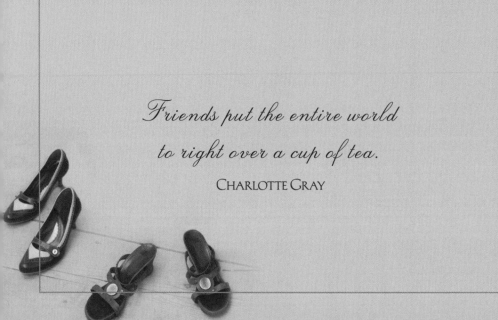

*Friends put the entire world
to right over a cup of tea.*

CHARLOTTE GRAY

$\mathcal{N}$o distance of place or lapse of time can lessen the friendship of those who are thoroughly persuaded of each other's worth.

ROBERT SOUTHEY

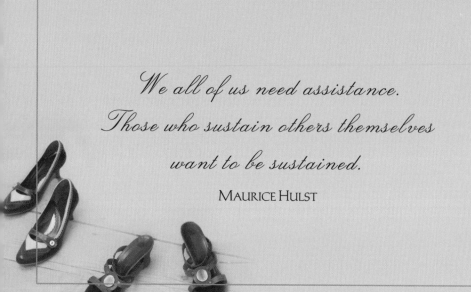

We all of us need assistance.
Those who sustain others themselves
want to be sustained.

MAURICE HULST

So long as we love, we serve; so long as we
are loved by others, I would say that we are indispensable;
and no man is useless while he has a friend.

ROBERT LOUIS STEVENSON

True friendship isn't measured by time,
but by the times shared.

KELLY EILEEN HAKE

There are two things one should know about the direction of life. First is: Where am I going? Second is: Who will go with me?

ELIE WIESEL

A friend is, as it were, a second self.

CICERO

Being confident of this, that he who began a good work in you will carry it on to completion until the day of Christ Jesus.

PHILIPPIANS 1:6 NIV

They may forget what you said,
but they will never forget
how you made them feel.

CARL W. BUECHNER

Friendship is born at the moment when
one person says to another: "What! You, too?
I thought I was the only one."

C. S. LEWIS

A friend is one who knows you and loves you just the same.

ELBERT HUBBARD

*G*od has paved our journey through the adventure of life. . . . Our friends are the flowers He planted along the way.

BONNIE JENSEN

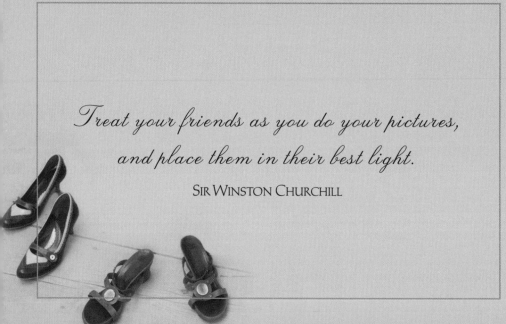

Treat your friends as you do your pictures,
and place them in their best light.

SIR WINSTON CHURCHILL

$\mathcal{T}$o have a good friend is one of the highest delights of life;
to be a good friend is one of the noblest undertakings.

UNKNOWN

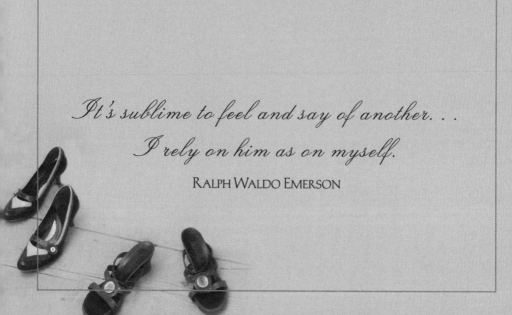

It's sublime to feel and say of another. . .
I rely on him as on myself.

RALPH WALDO EMERSON

The best and most beautiful things in the world cannot be seen or even touched. They must be felt with the heart.

HELEN KELLER

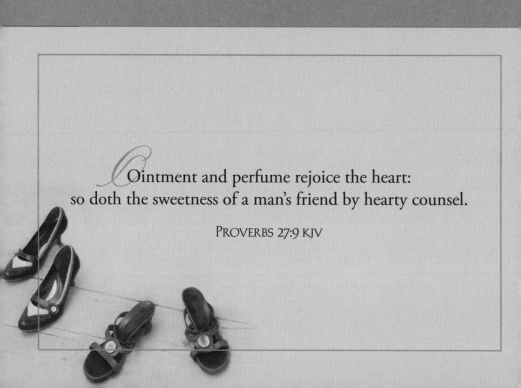

Ointment and perfume rejoice the heart:
so doth the sweetness of a man's friend by hearty counsel.

PROVERBS 27:9 KJV

I find true friendship to be. . .

the true. . .restorative cordial.

THOMAS JEFFERSON

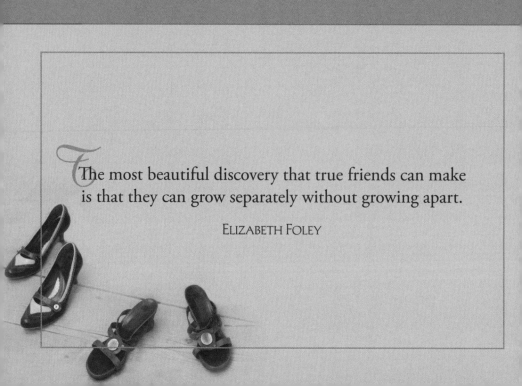

The most beautiful discovery that true friends can make
is that they can grow separately without growing apart.

ELIZABETH FOLEY

There is nothing on this earth more to be prized than true friendship.

Holding the heart of another in the comforting
hands of prayer is a priceless act of love.

JANET L. WEAVER

A faithful friend is an image of God.

FRENCH PROVERB

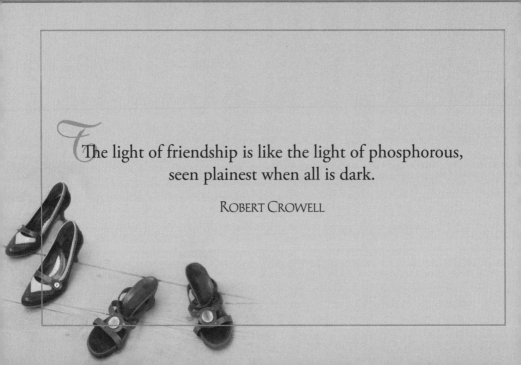

The light of friendship is like the light of phosphorous,
seen plainest when all is dark.

ROBERT CROWELL

Friends. . .they cherish one another's hopes.
They are kind to one another's dreams.

HENRY DAVID THOREAU

Without friends, no one would choose to live,
though he had all other goods.

ARISTOTLE

Dear friend, I pray that you may enjoy good health and that all may go well with you, even as your soul is getting along well.

3 JOHN 2 NIV

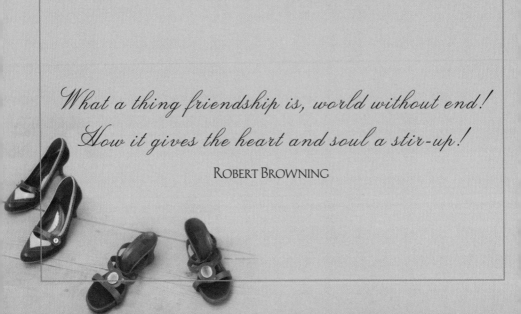

What a thing friendship is, world without end!

How it gives the heart and soul a stir-up!

ROBERT BROWNING

Two friends can be together in the silence with genuine
creativity in solace or joy or supplication.

EUGENIA PRICE

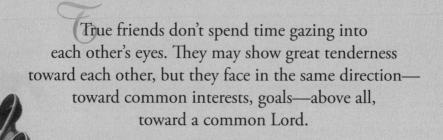

True friends don't spend time gazing into
each other's eyes. They may show great tenderness
toward each other, but they face in the same direction—
toward common interests, goals—above all,
toward a common Lord.

C. S. LEWIS

Walking with a friend in the dark is better than walking alone in the light.

HELEN KELLER

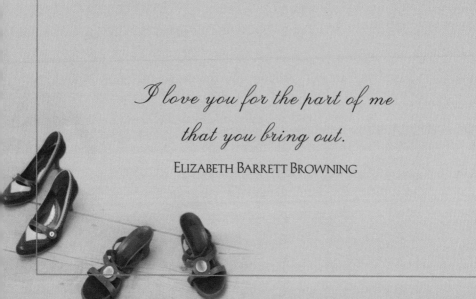

*I love you for the part of me
that you bring out.*

ELIZABETH BARRETT BROWNING

If you can eat today, enjoy the sunlight today,
mix good cheer with friends today,
enjoy it, and bless God for it.

HENRY WARD BEECHER

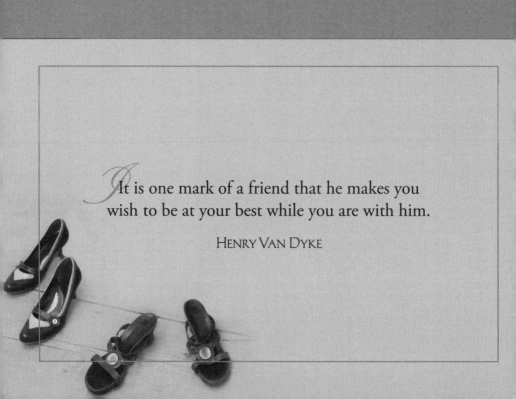

*I*t is one mark of a friend that he makes you
wish to be at your best while you are with him.

HENRY VAN DYKE

Your best friend is the person who brings out of you the best that is within you.

HENRY FORD

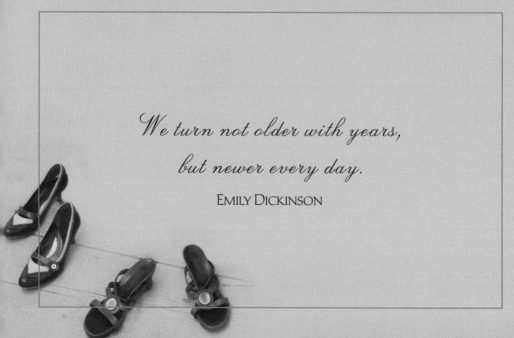

We turn not older with years,
but newer every day.

EMILY DICKINSON

May the blessing of light be on you,
light without and light within. . . . May the blessed sunshine
shine on you and warm your heart till it glows like a
great peat fire, so that the stranger may come and
warm himself at it, and also a friend.

TRADITIONAL IRISH BLESSING

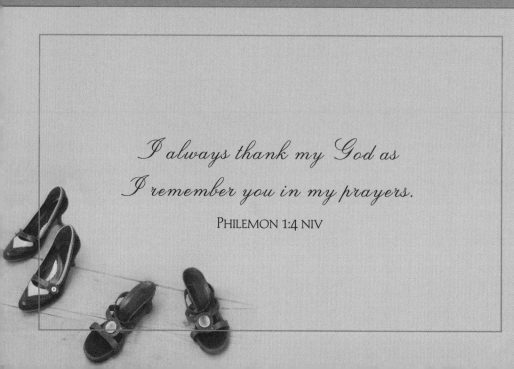

I always thank my God as
I remember you in my prayers.

PHILEMON 1:4 NIV

You know you've made a new friend when. . .
the differences you find only make the
other person seem more interesting.

ELLYN SANNA